A Prisoner of War's Story

STRATIS DOUKAS

A Prisoner of War's Story

Translated by
Petro Alexiou

With an Afterword by
Dimitris Tziovas

This translation has been assisted by the Federal Government of Australia through the Australia Council, its arts funding and advisory body.

We would like to thank Charalampos Minasidis for advice on historical matters, Katherine Demopoulos for her insightful editing and Professor Dimitris Tziovas for permission to include in this volume, as an afterword, the introduction he wrote for the first edition.

Petro Alexiou has studied literature, philosophy and history in Australia (where he was born) and Greece. From 1983-1996 he subtitled Greek films for Australia's public broadcaster SBS-TV. He has written scripts for film and video and has published children's stories and articles on Greek literature and cinema, as well as Greek-Australian history.

Original title: *Ιστορία ενός αιχμαλώτου*

© Aiora Press 2022

First edition published in 1999 by the Centre for Byzantine, Ottoman and Modern Greek Studies at the University of Birmingham, in its Birmingham Modern Greek Translations series.

Second revised edition published in October 2022 by Aiora Press. Reprinted July 2024.

All rights reserved. No part of this publication may be reproduced, stored in a retrieval system, or transmitted, in any form or by any means, electronic, mechanical, photocopying, recording or otherwise, without written permission of the publishers.

ISBN: 978-618-5369-66-8

AIORA PRESS
11 Mavromichali St.
Athens 10679 – Greece
tel: +30 210 3839000
www.aiorabooks.com

CONTENTS

Foreword 9

Map: Narrator's Journey 11

A Prisoner of War's Story 17

Background Note by the Author 83

Afterword 91

FOREWORD

Miletus, Ephesus, Halicarnassus, Pergamum, Magnesia, Meander and Smyrna—these are just a few of the ancient Greek cities that thrived for centuries on the Asia Minor coastline. Their names evoke a far distant past, but Greeks continued to live in the region for many centuries: in the Hellenistic age, when Greek language and culture spread widely; in the Roman and Byzantine periods; and then in the years of the Ottoman Empire, when Greeks and Turks lived in the same land, all subjects of the sultan in a multi-ethnic state.

In the early twentieth century, however, the Young Turk Revolution led to a nationalist turn within the crumbling Ottoman Empire. During the First World War, persecutions, deportations and massacres occurred against non-Muslim minorities, mainly Armenians, Greeks and Assyrians. In 1919, at the end of the war, with the Ottoman state on the losing side and under harsh mandates, Greece was authorized by the Allies to send troops to Smyrna, on the Aegean coast of Anatolia, to secure order and protect the ethnic Greek population. Facing growing Turkish resistance, the Greek army advanced deep into the hinterland and was eventually defeated by Kemal Ataturk's forces. In 1922, after more than thirty centuries of Greek presence in Asia Minor, more than one million Greeks fled across the Aegean. The Asia Minor Disaster culminated in cosmopolitan Smyrna in flames.

The narrator in *A Prisoner of War's Story* is a young Anatolian Greek who fought in the Ottoman army during the First World War and also, on his account, the Greek army of occupation during the Asia Minor campaign. By September 1922, the Turkish nationalist army was mobilizing all Ottoman Greek males above the age of fifteen and sending them to labour battalions, regardless of whether they had fought with the Greek army. The narrator is one of these men.

A Prisoner of War's Story

*Dedicated to the common ordeals
of people everywhere*

At the Smyrna disaster I was with my parents on the harbour front at Punta. I was dragged away from them. And I was left behind in Turkey, a prisoner.

It was midday when I was taken away with the others. Night fell and the patrols were still bringing men to the barracks. Near midnight the guards came in. We were crammed up against one another and they started hitting us right and left with sticks, kicking those of us who were sitting on the ground, our knees drawn up. Then they picked out as many as they wanted and led them away, cursing as they went.

We were scared they'd do away with us all.

One of the clerks, who had his office beside the door, had heard us talking pitifully and beckoned to us.

'The next time they come and start calling out, stay at the back,' he said. 'But not a word to anyone else!'

From that night on, they took people from the barrack rooms every night. When we heard gunfire from Kadife Kalesi we said to each other, 'It's only firing practice.'

After days spent in fear, an officer came with forty soldiers and took charge of us. They took us out into the yard and separated us from the civilians. That's when I saw my brother. They put us in lines of four and ordered us to kneel so they could count us.

The officer, who was mounted on his horse, looked us over and said, 'I'll see to it that your seed is wiped out!'

Then he gave the order to march.

There must have been about two thousand men in our column.

They marched us straight to the marketplace. A Turkish mob was waiting there and, like a horde, fell on us. From all sides they attacked us with tables, chairs, glasses—whatever they could lay their hands on. There were European sailors with them in the cafés and they were looking on for a bit of fun.

When we reached Basmahane, a *hafiz*, a reciter of the Koran, came out and stood in front of us. He looked at us.

'Allah! Allah! What's going on?' he called out to the *asker aga*, the officer in command. The officer stopped.

'Captain, over here!' he called again.

Clip clop, the captain's horse came over. The captain saluted him.

'Is this what our Book says?' the *hafiz* asked him.

The captain saluted him again.

And we passed before them in lines.

At midday we reached Halkapinar. There they fenced around us with wire. When night fell, an *efe*, a Turkish armed leader from our village, came. He called to us by name, pretending he was going to save us, but his aim was to do us in. And we fell to the ground so he wouldn't recognize us.

At dawn another officer came from Magnesia and we were ordered to our feet. We walked for hours. We didn't know where they were taking us. But we could tell from the lie of the land that we were heading for Magnesia.

Instead of taking us along the main road they forced us up through the mountains. And as we weren't on the flat, we began to scatter. We couldn't keep to our lines of four and the soldiers kept shouting orders:

'Lines of four! Lines of four!'

We tried, but they kept on breaking up. Those who were weak and fell behind were dragged into the forest by civilians and done away with.

After a hard slog we met up with the main road. Again there were mobs waiting for us: old men, sixty to eighty years of age, carrying ancient daggers, and as we approached they ran towards us shouting at the captain:

'Let us do what we want with them!'

'No,' the captain told them, laughing.

We cried out to him, 'Captain, our lives are in your hands!'

And we moved on.

The roads on both sides were strewn with stinking corpses. At the springs, there were guards stationed by the fountains from whose spouts water ran. At the sight of them we felt even thirstier.

Many had died of thirst on the road. I was walking with my brother who was carrying a haversack belonging to one of our guards.

'We've got money,' I thought. 'Why not pay for some water?'

'I'm thirsty, I'll die,' I said to my brother.

'Don't lose heart,' he said to me. 'If they see we have money they'll do us in.'

'I can't stand it any more. Give them some money for a drink.'

He gave me some money and I ran straight to the Turk.

'Some water, I'm dying,' I said to him.

'What's that, you dog? You won't get a drop out of me!'

'*Asker aga*, it will be an act of charity. Here, take this money, too.'

'Hand it over,' he said to me. 'And don't let anyone see you.'

I drank and gave some to my brother.

This was in the month of August.[1]

Finally, one night, we reached the outskirts of Magnesia. People were waiting for us with clubs in hand.

'The prisoners are coming!' they shouted and ran towards us.

'Keep back!' the captain said to them. 'When we were doing the fighting you were all having a good time.'

They scattered, shouting out that one day the Yunanlilar, the Greeks, would try to do away with them again.

The captain, annoyed, rounded us up like sheep in a fold and set sentries around us. No water, bread—nothing!

Those who had money gave it to the guards for water. My companions gave money to a darky[2] and he brought us a full bucket.

'Be quick,' he said. 'The captain won't allow it.'

---

[1] September in the Gregorian calendar of modern times.

[2] (Greek *arapis*) Sometimes used for 'Arabic' but also anyone dark skinned, usually of African descent. Historically, it was used to varying degrees in a derogatory way, and its contemporary forms are invariably racist.

I drank and drank... My brother pulled me away so he could drink. Then the others rushed to get at the bucket and the water spilt.

The next morning it was still dark when the captain shouted, 'Get ready!'

We got into lines of four and moved off. He marched us into Magnesia. There he put us in some hospital grounds set amongst pine trees, enclosed with railings. He handed us over to a corporal. We were so tired we didn't feel hungry. But we were dying of thirst. We lay like the sick, and chewed on green pine needles under the trees. When a few clouds showed in the sky we prayed for rain. The clouds thickened and grew darker. They hung low in the sky, then slowly disappeared again. The sun burned hotter now.

'Water! Water!' we shouted in desperation.

But no one listened.

Five hours later, a fair-headed, well-dressed *hodja* came and with one voice we begged him: '*Hodja, Allah askina!* For the love of Allah! We're thirsty! Water!'

He seemed to take pleasure in seeing us in our sorry state: 'That's how I want to see you till the end, creeping and crawling like snakes.' And off he went.

Then another *hodja* came in a buggy. Once again we called out: '*Allah askina*, some water! We're thirsty. We can't bear it!'

After having a good look at us, he said, 'I've had my bit of fun.' And he ordered his driver to move on.

Seven days went by like this. Those of us who had money drank water. The others drank their own piss.

Many died of hunger and thirst. The guards told us to form a fatigue party to get rid of the bodies. We fought over who would go because the fatigue party would get to drink water. About twenty men took them in carts and threw them away, far from town.

In the hospital grounds there were some prisoners from Magnesia who told us that the fountain in the yard held water. We didn't believe them.

That night we were woken by shouting and learnt that the Magnesians had broken the pipe and found water. We got up and scrambled to get to it. The sentries heard the noise and began to fire on us. After quite a few bodies had fallen they fenced us in with barbed wire. We took handfuls of mud and sucked on it.

After seven days one of the *hodjas* returned. We cried out, begging him for help.

'Quiet or I'm leaving!' he said. 'I've come to save you.'

As he spoke they brought us rations of dry bread in baskets. They put us in single file and gave half a loaf to every two men. Then they let us drink in turn at the fountain.

The soldiers told us that an important man had come that very day from Ahmetli: 'From now on you'll be treated well.'

In the evening they stripped us bare! They took whatever we had: rings, watches. Even our gold teeth.

They roused us in the morning. As we were getting ready, a group of Zeybeks[3] with their reed pipes and drums gathered outside. They set to beating us with their rifles as we walked out through the barbed wire fencing. Another officer came. He took charge of us and we moved off.

About three hours' march from Magnesia we came to a large vineyard surrounded by a fence. The officer placed us there until daybreak, with sentries guarding us.

We scattered amongst the harvested vines and ate the leaves with our bread.

When night fell, two men tried to escape. The sentries caught them and shot them in front of us.

In the morning, the captain said to us, 'Infidel dogs! I try to help you and you run off?'

He ordered his men to get us to our feet.

We marched for hours. At a railway station where we stopped, some Turkish civilians came and asked the officer to let them search amongst us. If they found the man they were looking for they wanted to take him.

---

[3] A warlike people in the Smyrna and Aydin districts, believed to have originally been Greek settlers from Thrace who converted to Islam. In earlier times they served as troops for local rulers. Their resort to brigandage added to a fearsome reputation.

'Yes,' he said. 'Have a look and if you find him, take him.'

'*Aferim! Aferim!* Bravo! Bravo!' they shouted and entered the throng. They did find him. He was an Armenian, the station gardener.

'Hey, you Armenian bastard! You're the one we're looking for.'

'What do you want from me?' he said. 'I only have one life to lose.'

And he passed amongst us, head held high, as though wanting everyone to see him.

'Take him away!' the captain shouted.

When the Armenian heard this he threw himself at the man who had first laid hands on him and in a frenzy bit his throat.

The others did away with the Armenian on the spot. All he had time to say was, 'Do what you want with me; I've taken my blood.'

Leaving behind the warm corpse, which they were still kicking about, we set off for Kasaba. There everything was burnt to the ground. They put us in a stockyard. From there we could see other prisoners being marched away, and hearing their tormented cries from afar we thanked the Lord.

In the morning they marched us towards Ahmetli. When we arrived, the captain was waiting for us at the railway station and he told us we'd be staying there.

He took us to a barren patch of ground and left us in the sun. We begged him to put us on the other side where there were trees.

'No. In the sun,' he said and left.

In the afternoon it rained. We were glad. We drank water in cupped hands, washed and felt refreshed.

When night fell, the captain came and put us under a shelter. Dawn found us still on our feet. It had rained all night.

The captain came back in the morning. He had a clerk with him. The captain divided us into companies and picked out the tradesmen: about ten bakers and dough kneaders, twenty carpenters and blacksmiths and the same number of masons and plasterers. As he sorted them, he said, 'You destroyed everything, now build it again.'

And he handed them over to the soldiers.

The clerk called out, 'Isn't there a miller amongst you? We have grain to grind. Doesn't any one of you know a miller's work?'

My brother and two others stepped forward.

The bakers went to the bakery and made some loaves out of unsifted barley. From then on we were each issued a quarter of a loaf every day. One night two bakers stole some dough. They'd planned to escape. The sentry caught them in the act. In the morning the guards took them to the captain who was lodging in a hut nearby.

'These men stole dough last night so they could escape,' the guards said to him.

The captain took out his pistol.

'Whoever does such things will die like a dog,' he said and shot them in front of us. Then he put us on fatigue to clean up the station. Our eyes stung from the filth.

A sergeant called Turan, who was guarding us, set to shouting and beating us so that the women in the train passing by would admire him. If anyone's eyes were hurting badly he'd say he was taking them to the hospital for treatment but instead he'd drag them into a ditch and do away with them.

One night the captain ordered the guards to tell the neighbouring villages that whoever wanted farmhands could come and get them.

'Tell them we've got everything: shepherds, masons, blacksmiths, whatever they want.'

In the morning the village headmen came and began to choose, first fifty then eighty, as many as they wanted, as though we were beasts.

We decided—twelve of us from my village—to wait till we heard of a good village, and when they came and asked for more men we'd all go together.

A few days later, a corporal, who liked us because we'd given him a belt he'd taken a fancy to when we were first captured, said to us, 'Be ready to go. There's a good village close by, Pinarbasi near Mount Boz. You'll be treated well.'

We asked him if he'd be coming with us.

'No,' he said. 'The captain won't let me. I'll hand you over to the headman.'

He handed us over and we left.

As we walked along the road we saw a wild pear tree and fell upon the unripe fruit.

'Hey, come on,' the headman called to us. 'It'll be night soon.'

We walked on again, eating as we went.

We reached the village at night. We were separated, four of us to each of three different places.

We worked twenty days in that place and from the day we got there we set our minds on escaping. We began secretly putting aside bread for the road and whatever else from our food that would keep.

Finally we settled on the day. We'd set off on Friday, at midnight. When the time came I woke my companion and everyone in turn woke each other. But the others had second thoughts.

'We've made our minds up,' we said to them. 'We're leaving.'

And we left.

After we'd walked for an hour or so from the village we came to the edge of a cliff overhanging a stream. The stream was so far down we couldn't hear its roar. We came to a stop.

There was a village close by. The dogs caught our scent and started barking.

'They'll find us,' I said to my companion. 'We'll have to cross tonight.'

'Yes,' he said.

Hugging the rocks and crawling along, we started down. But we couldn't go on. Halfway down we stopped at a cave. We waited there till dawn.

When day broke we heard voices on the clifftop. The whole village was at our heels, hunting us with their dogs.

Their voices slowly faded into the distance. We stayed for a while, hidden, then began to climb down the cliff again.

It was almost midday by the sun when we reached the bottom of the hollow.

'Lord!' we said when we saw the side we had to climb up. We walked for a while, upright, alongside the bubbling waters. Then we entered, treading carefully on the slippery pebbles. The water came up to our knees.

As we waded on we heard a rattling sound close by. We were frightened. We drew close together and looked about. Above us, some ravens were flying low, in circles. We bent down and drank some water, though we weren't thirsty. Then we left the stream, dripping wet and began to climb.

The sun was going down as we scaled the cliff,

hanging onto clumps of weeds. With great difficulty we made it to the top. The dark had overtaken us.

When we got to even ground we looked about. In front of us, a little distance away, were some shepherd's huts. They belonged to Yuruks.[4] Their dogs started barking.

The shepherds called to each other: 'The dogs are barking. There are people about.' And they fired their rifles into the air.

We turned towards the cliff and walked along the edge, bending low, until we came to an abandoned village. As we walked through the ruins we heard a whimper a few feet ahead of us. We drew nearer.

A dog was lying on a mattress that was spilling its straw.

When the dog saw us it tried to stand up but it couldn't. It wagged its tail on the ground, blinked its eyes, which shone in the moonlight, and whimpered once again. We sat down next to it, leaning against a low wall in the crumbling yard. Featherless hens, dried up with thirst, roosted on piles of broken things. We thought of making off with one but were afraid to light a fire. We looked at the dog again, then set off. We walked all night in the moonlight, startled by our own shadows.

---

[4] (Turkish *yürük*). A term referring to pastoral nomadic peoples, mostly descendants of the Turkoman tribe.

Towards dawn we reached the Mount Boz pastures where goats were grazing. A woman was tending them. We hurried to get past but didn't make it. The herd surrounded us. The woman was stooped over, knitting. She didn't notice us. We passed by.

On the fourth day we reached Odemis. On our way we came upon a mill.

'Hey,' I said to my companion. 'We can't just keep walking on and on like this.' And I motioned towards the mill.

'What?' he said. 'Break in?'

We both agreed but then changed our minds.

Afterwards we came to a main road and went into the forest to hide. Around midday we saw a hunter on the opposite ridge. His dog was barking. We were afraid. We crawled along about ten metres and lay low behind a tree trunk waiting for the hunter to go. We got tired from waiting. He stayed till late at night. Then, crossing ourselves, we started out.

Before dawn we reached the outskirts of the town of Banos. Its olive groves stretched almost as far as Bayindir. We were so hungry we set to eating the green olives, which left a bitter taste in our mouths.

After we'd eased our hunger a little, we stood there looking at the town. Opposite us was the railway line. The train came and went two or three times. The people who got off scattered onto the roads. We couldn't get through. It was getting dark and the roads were still full of people. We left late in the night.

We passed Bayindir quickly and reached the Meander river. The water came up to our waists. We crossed over.

As we stepped out, we saw sheep. We couldn't turn back; we stumbled into the flock. The dogs rushed at us and we kept them at bay with our staffs. They kept at us. We calmed them down and, bending low, slowly withdrew.

After we'd left the flock a good way behind, we sat down. We couldn't take another step. Even a small child could have caught us.

Finally we reached the outskirts of our village. We went into the forest and from there we could see the village on the hilltop, just as we'd known it. There were about fifty lights burning. Dogs were barking. It was just as we had left it. We wept. We felt like deserters returning from war to the peace of our homes.

'Let's go,' my companion said. 'Our people may still be there. Let's go and see for ourselves.'

We set off separately after arranging to meet the next day at the cave. We headed for different neighbourhoods. Wherever we went we found everything in ruins. The houses open, empty, the doors smashed with axes. There were only a few Turks still living around the square and a sentry was posted at the police station. Inside the school, where they'd piled up clothes and furniture, voices could be heard.

I drew back and wandered about all night, fear my only companion.

When we met in the morning we broke down and cried. We had counted on finding at least something left behind by our people in the village. But we'd found nothing and in desperation we raided the fig orchards.

With the rain, most of the figs had rotted but the chestnuts and the olives were ripening.

We gathered as much fruit as we could and took it to our cave.

One day as we sat outside looking at a mill opposite, I said to my companion, 'No matter how much I eat I still feel dizzy. Why don't we keep a watch near the mill and break in when the miller leaves?'

'Let's do that,' he said. And we went and set up our watch.

The miller's customers came and went. When night fell, the miller mounted his horse and he too went.

We waited till midnight just in case someone else might still be inside or the miller himself returned. There was no sign of anyone.

We crossed ourselves and set out.

The lock was broken but the door was barred from the inside. We got in from the northern side where the water flowed out. An oil lamp burned by the mouth of the oven. We took fright. But then we said, 'Better to eat some bread, even if we die.' We looked in the cupboard. There was a crock with oil, some tomatoes and salt. In a basket were two pitta breads. Pots were lying upside down on the window sill. We made a salad and ate.

We gave thanks to God as though He were there before us and we talked eagerly. We felt consoled.

Then we got up and searched everywhere. In a nook we found about twenty church candles. We took them. We found some flour and half a sack of wheat in a barrel. We emptied it out to grind it. We let the water through and the mill began to grind.

It was almost dawn. We gathered whatever else we needed, filled two sacks with flour and headed for the forest. There we lay in wait, to see what would happen.

At daybreak the miller came with some Yuruk customers.

As soon as they went inside we heard shouting. The miller cursed, thinking he'd been robbed by his own people.

We kept watch till midday. When we saw it was quiet, we went to the cave to sort out the things we'd taken from the mill. We'd made good provision: oil, flour and salt, aubergines and tomatoes from the surrounding gardens. At night we'd cook in the cave, browning dough cakes on the red-hot coals. In the morning we'd take our food and go off into the forest where we'd stay till nightfall.

One day as we sat in hiding, a Yuruk appeared before us holding a double-barrelled shotgun. He stared at us. We were terrified. We thought he was a watchman.

'Where are you from, countrymen?' he asked.

'From Macedonia,' we said. '*Muhajir*.[5] Refugees. The government has sent us here, to Savirkoy. This is our land now. What are you doing here?'

'I was just passing by and came to gather some chestnuts. The *giaours*[6] have gone now,' he said and went on his way.

When he was out of sight we looked at each other.

'The sun has set,' I said to my companion. 'Let's go.'

On our way we came across a country chapel. We entered and knelt to pray, hoping a saint might appear and hear our woes. We saw nothing. Only bare walls and boards.

Deep in thought we returned to our den. We didn't sleep all night out of fear that they'd come and catch us in our sleep. This wasn't the only thing that tormented us. The itching from the lice didn't leave us a moment's peace. We would have preferred hunger to putting up with them.

---

[5] (Turkish *muhacir*). An emigrant or refugee. In this context, a Muslim who has immigrated from a Balkan country into an area under Ottoman rule.

[6] (Turkish *gâvur*). A derogatory term for non-Muslims, especially Christians. The term may imply obstinacy, fanaticism, irreligion or cruelty.

So in the morning we decided to go down to the stream below the cave. It was still twilight when we got there and made a fire out of dry wood. While we waited for the water to boil we cut our hair and shaved our beards with a razor and scissors we'd found in the village. Then we stripped and scalded our clothes.

That day we got some peace. Two days later the lice were back again. We scalded them every day until we were finally free of them.

Then the flour ran out. We'd eaten almost forty *okas*[7] of bread in as many days. On the road, further down from us, was another mill. 'A hungry dog can find its way into a bakehouse,' as they say. We decided to go to this one, too, and began to keep a lookout. But the miller lived there. Finally, one day he left for the village in the company of three others. Night fell but the roads were still busy.

It was midnight and the miller had not yet appeared. We decided he wasn't coming so we approached the mill. We listened from outside. No voice could be heard. We tried to open the door. It seemed to be firmly shut from within. We decided to enter through the bakehouse, which had a window.

'You keep watch on the road,' I said to my companion. 'If you see anyone, give me a signal.'

---

[7] (Greek οκά from Turkish *okka*). A Turkish measure of weight equal to 1.28 kilograms.

I broke the glass and climbed inside. A basket above the window fell. I froze. 'The miller!' I thought, trembling. But my hunger was stronger than my fear. I went downstairs and opened up. My companion entered and closed the door again. We lit a lamp and searched everywhere. In a cupboard we found two loaves of bread and a pot of cooked beans. On the shelf there was some soap, tobacco and a belt, which I tied around my waist. Behind the door, in a pannier, were some dirty clothes and next to it a sack of flour and another of wheat. We gathered everything up, the pot of food as well, and left. Our cave was close to the mill and bit by bit we carried it all up.

The next morning, before dawn, we went to a spot opposite the mill and watched. The miller came on his own and, cursing, left for the village. Not half an hour went by before a detachment of cavalry came along the road. In our fear, we spent the rest of the day hiding in the cave.

The next day at dawn, we took some bread and left. We did this for almost a week. No one came. We became less afraid.

Below our cave were some enormous olive trees. They were so dense that the sunlight never reached their trunks. One night we went into the grove to pick olives. While we were picking we heard voices.

I drew near to my companion: 'There are people about, we must hide.'

I'd hardly spoken when about two metres away some men and women, Yuruks, appeared on the road. As they passed our tree one of the men said, 'I'll bet you anything that there are still *giaours* around here.'

When they'd gone my companion said to me, 'We'll have to change our hiding place.' And taking precautions we returned to our cave.

We couldn't eat that night. We lay down to sleep, fearful that we'd be caught.

At daybreak, we gathered our things and went further away to another cave that we knew. There, we made ourselves more comfortable. It was deep and about two metres wide. We'd found a kneading trough and two empty olive oil cans in the village. We had lots of olives. We crushed them to a pulp, put them in a feedbag and poured boiling water over them, pressing them thoroughly in the trough. Then we poured the oily water into a can in the base of which we'd made a hole. The water slowly drained away, leaving the oil behind. That day we cooked and, after eating our fill, lay down. The light shone far into the cave, making the spiders move about on their webs. We were glad of their company.

We lived for four whole months in there.

Then one morning, as I was chanting hymns, reading from a breviary I'd found in the village, my companion prodded me and said, 'Hush! I hear voices.'

He stared out from the depths of the cave.

In front of it, about ten feet away, there was a path. Footsteps approached. The cave sucked in the conversation like a vortex.

'Our cattle must be around here...'

Then they came into sight. They were two Yuruk cowherds. We made ready with cudgels in our hands. If they saw us, we'd kill them.

They didn't see us. They passed by peacefully, talking, their hands clasped behind their backs.

My companion said to me once again, 'We have to leave this place, too.'

'But where else can we go?' I answered him.

'I'm not staying,' he said. 'They may have seen something and gone straight to the garrison.'

'All right,' I said. 'We'll do as you say.'

And we set off to find a new hideout. We searched till evening. We found one, another cave, at a spot called Aghia Triada. We carted our things there in the night.

We were so scared we didn't go outside for ten days. Day by day our supplies were running lower. Finally we had nothing to eat. We were dizzy with hunger.

'I can't stand it any longer,' I said to my companion. 'Why don't we kill the miller?'

'Don't say that!' he said to me. 'Do you want to damn your soul? The crops, the chickpeas... they'll soon be ready. We'll have food to eat again.'

'What we've been eating up to now hasn't done much for us,' I replied. 'We can't just live on grass. Either we find something to eat or else we go to Smyrna and give ourselves up.'

'No,' he said. 'I won't hand myself over to the Turk. I'd rather die here in this cave.'

'Don't think like that,' I said to him. 'It's a city. They can't kill us there.'

'No,' he replied. 'Never.'

'Let's do something else then,' I said. 'We'll make out we're Turks. We'll go down and find work. Our fate is written. Whatever is to happen will happen.'

'Agreed,' he said.

'But we can't go together,' I said to him. 'We'll give ourselves away with our talk.'

So we decided to separate. We'd go to different villages.

'What place do you know well?' I asked him.

'Aydin,' he said.

'All right,' I said. 'I know Thira well. I can work as a shepherd there. I'm good with animals.'

And we agreed that in two months, if no one found us out, we'd meet at Thira or the sheepfolds.

'That is, if we don't come to harm,' he said as he looked out at the dark shadows entering our cave like smoke.

In the dead of night the rain came pelting down. We thought the lightning would split the cave apart.

We set to talking in the dark. There was nothing we didn't talk about. Finally, we turned to our parting. We'd decide and change our minds. We'd decide again, and again we'd change our minds.

With the first light of day my friend rose and took out his razor. He gave it a good stropping on his belt and smiled bitterly.

'Come on. Don't just stand there,' he said to me and he turned my neck to the side.

He shaved me, then I shaved him. We stared at each other.

'Do I look like a Turk?' I asked him.

'A real Mehmet.'

'And you look like a Cretan Turk.'[8]

'Let's get going. We've wasted away.'

We grasped each other by the hand and wouldn't let go. We thought we'd never see each other again. We wept and made our peace. Then we each took our fated road. As we went our ways, we kept looking back. In the end, he disappeared from sight.

'Fool!' I said to myself and almost ran after him. But my heart said no. I always listened to my heart. That was my way.

---

[8] Crete was occupied by the Ottomans in 1669. In the late nineteenth century with Crete's growing autonomy, half of the island's 70,000 Muslims emigrated to Asia Minor.

I walked freely on, putting my fears aside. Having made my decision, I approached some Yuruks sitting around a fire close by. I knew them from before. One was called Behchet Ali. 'They're Yuruks, simple people,' I thought and walked up to them with a greeting.

'*Selam aleykum.* Peace be with you.'

'*Aleykum selam,*' they replied.

'What are you doing here?' I asked them.

'Grazing camels.'

'Where are you from?'

'We're not from here. We're living in tents below the stream.'

'I'm a stranger, too,' I said. 'Could you show me the road to Tire.'[9]

'The plain has flooded. The roads are impassable.'

'Which way should I go, then?' I asked.

---

[9] Turkish name for the town the Greeks called Thira.

'That way. Don't go past the huts, there are dogs.'
'Good night to you,' I said.
'Godspeed,' they said.
And I set off.
When I reached the peak of the ridge the dogs caught my scent. I quickly climbed a boulder and began to shout loudly.

'*Hemsheri! Hemsheri*! Compatriot! Compatriot!'

A man lighting a fire in front of his hut pretended he couldn't hear me. Finally he came over. He chased the dogs away and took me back to the hut.

'*Buyurun*, come in,' he said. 'Where have you come from?'

'Aydin,' I said. 'I'm on my way to Tepekoy to look for work. What can a poor man do?'

'You must be hungry,' he said and placed a bowl with yoghurt and bread before me.

As I ate I questioned him about those parts pretending I didn't know them.

'You'll go down to Halka first and then on to Tepekoy. You can't go directly to Tire from here.'

When I'd eaten and thanked him I bid him good night.

'Godspeed,' he said and looked up at the sky, which was preparing a downpour. He was about to say something but then leant over the fire, rubbing his palms together above the flames.

I left, tapping on the rocks with my wooden staff.

I had walked some distance when I came upon a

destroyed Turkish village. Smoke was rising out of a house half in ruins. I wondered who was inside. Man or woman? I paused to take a look.

No sooner had I stopped than two soldiers rushed out.

I was scared they'd ask for identity papers, but they took off, running towards Belhem.

I waited a while then entered. They had lit a fire in the fireplace to dry themselves out from the rain. I warmed myself and looked around in the ruins at the walls with their strips of coloured wallpaper. Then I left.

A little way ahead of me five or six women were walking. Their clothes looked as though they were made from the cloth of my village.

A shiver ran down my spine. 'Fellow villagers!' I thought and hurriedly overtook them.

They spread out on the col below, picking wild greens. Nearby a man was ploughing. I greeted him.

'*Kuvvet ola!* Good strength to you!' I said.

'*Eyvallah*. Thank you,' he replied.

I went on my way.

Further along I came to a main road. An old man was riding past on his horse. I had known him six years earlier when I was a soldier.[10] He was a well-to-do

---

[10] As a Greek Ottoman citizen, the narrator in 1916 was most likely

camel farmer. I thought to myself, 'He won't recognize me after all this time.' I approached him without fear.

'*Selam aleykum,*' I said.

'*Aleykum selam,*' he replied indifferently.

We continued on our way. I walked behind him and to the side.

'Tell me,' he said suddenly. 'Where are you from?'

'From Bursa,' I replied.

'The city itself?'

'No. A village called Kestel.'

'Where are you going now?'

'To Tire, to town.'

'What's your line of work?'

'I'm a shepherd.'

'Do you have work?'

'No,' I replied.

'Come and work for me. I have camels.'

'I don't know anything about camels. If you had sheep I'd come.'

'You'll learn. You'll get used to it.'

'How can I learn?' I said to him. 'A poor fellow like me?'

'Oh well, *uyurlar olsun,* good luck,' he said.

'Godspeed,' I said to him.

As I followed behind, I was plagued by the fear he might recognize me.

---

conscripted into the Ottoman Army to fight in the First World War.

A little way along he turned onto a path. I continued walking briskly, as though in a hurry to reach home.

Across from me, on a hillock in the distance, a Turk was ploughing. Before I drew near he left his oxen and began to pray. I surveyed the sky, waiting for my moment. When he'd finished I went up to him. We greeted each other in the customary way.

'Where are you going?' he asked.

'Tire,' I said.

'Stay here tonight, my friend. You won't make it, it's getting dark. There's a storm brewing. My village is over there. There's a guest room. Stay the night and tomorrow you can be on your way. Wait a while and we'll go together.'

'No, thank you,' I said. 'I'm in a hurry to catch a train. Tomorrow I'm leaving for Bayindir.'

'You'll be a laughing stock if you go to town in the state you're in. Stay the night and we'll see.'

'No, my friend, I'd best be on my way.'

Then I left because we had once been near neighbours and I was afraid he'd recognize me.

About an hour later it began to rain. I was soaked, dripping wet. Alone on the road in the dark I was filled with despair. I felt like grabbing a rock and beating my head with it. I hit myself with my fists and wept.

Night had fallen when I reached the edge of a village. It was called Sipni. A shepherd was driving his flock to the fold. I joined him and lent a hand. When we reached the fold we exchanged greetings.

'*Merhaba.*'

'Where are you going?' he asked.

'To town,' I said.

'Godspeed,' he said and shut the gate of the sheepfold.

'Please, friend,' I begged him. 'We are of one faith. Let me stay the night and I'll leave in the morning.'

'I can't,' he said. 'I'm just a hand.'

'Ask your master, then.'

'It's the womenfolk,' he replied. 'The men are away. In the time of the Greeks they were guides and Kemal put them in prison.'[11]

'What does it matter if they are women? I won't eat them. And I don't need any bread. Just a corner to spend the night.'

'It doesn't bother me, friend,' he said. 'I can sleep in the open under my cape.'

He went to the womenfolk and asked them and they said yes.

'Come inside,' he said to me, pleased with himself.

I entered and closed the gate.

---

[11] A reference to the previous three years when the Greek army occupied part of Anatolia, beginning with its landing at Smyrna on 15 May 1919. Mustafa Kemal (later Atatürk) was leader of the rebel government and founder of the Turkish republic.

In a little while other shepherds came. They lit a fire and as we sat around it they asked me where I was from and where I was bound.

'I'm from Aydin and I'm looking for work.'

'What work do you do?'

'I'm a shepherd. I'd like to stay here with you.'

'There's nothing for you to do here. There are three of us. If you want work you'll find it at Tepekoy. Go there in the morning.'

They put food on the table for all of us to eat.

'I'm shivering,' I said. 'I can't.'

'Warm up by the fire, then eat,' they said. 'You can sleep here next to us.'

As we were eating I saw a trunk filled with clothes that didn't look as though they belonged to the sheepfold. I asked them where they had come from.

'Not far from here there was a rich village, Kirkidze. When the *giaours* left we took everything. Everything you see here was theirs.'

'That was a godsend,' I said to them. 'But why didn't they burn it down?'

'Other villages were burnt to ashes,' they said. 'Didn't you get anything?'

'No, I was fighting. I didn't steal, but I did kill.'

'You did better than us,' they said and moved away from the fire. 'Here, take this cape and lie down.'

I lay down next to them. I didn't sleep all night for fear I might say something in my sleep.

It was still dark when I got up.

'What's the hurry?' they said to me. 'Stay and have something to eat before you leave.'

'No,' I said. 'I'd best be on my way. If you could spare me a little bread...' Then I bade them goodbye.

I set off down the road. From behind, about fifty cavalrymen approached singing. I stood to the side and waved to them as they passed. I followed close after them, seeing the clouds darkening. I ran and ducked inside a hut. The rain came down harder. I took the bread out of my bag. They'd put in some cheese. As I was eating I saw an armed horseman galloping straight towards the hut. I was frightened.

He drew up and greeted me. It was a watchman.

'Where have you come from?' he asked.

'I'm on my way to Tire to find work. The rain held me up.'

'What work do you do?'

'I'm a shepherd.'

'There are sheepfolds at Tire,' he said and gave me some tobacco to roll a cigarette.

'You wouldn't know of a good sheepfold around here, would you?' I asked him.

'Over there at Hadji Mehmet's,' he said. 'He's a good master—you'll be treated well. So long,' he said and dug his knees into the horse's flanks.

When the rain stopped I headed straight for a flock of sheep. The shepherd came over to me.

'What do you want?' he asked.

'I'm looking for work,' I said.

Immediately I regretted it. I realized from his speech that he was an Arvanitis[12] and I didn't want to stay with them because they were sharp—I wanted Turks; I knew them. I didn't stop to talk and kept along the path towards the sound of bells. In the distance I saw another large flock of sheep slowly descending as they grazed on a slope amongst some olive trees.

When I drew near I called out to the shepherd because the dogs had begun to bark. The shepherd came towards me as I walked, until we met. We greeted each other.

'Whose sheep are they?' I asked.

'Hadji Mehmet's,' he said, just as the watchman had told me.

'Your master wouldn't be looking for a shepherd, would he?'

'He's been going to Tire every day now for a week looking for an apprentice and still hasn't found one. If you like, wait till he comes. Do you know the work?'

'I know how to milk and graze.'

---

[12] (Greek, plural Arvanites). Descendants of Albanians (originally ancient Illyrians) who settled in Greece and Asia Minor during the Byzantine and Ottoman periods.

'Take the flock, then, and graze them until he comes. Let them loose in the broad-bean patch. The master said to graze them there today.'

I left, whistling at the flock. The sheep obeyed me as if they knew me.

About midday I saw Hadji Mehmet approaching on his horse. Sitting astride his saddle he looked like a rich man. I was afraid of him. The shepherd went up and helped him dismount. As he stood and surveyed the flock passing before him, he said to the shepherd, 'Hasan, they look different to how I left them. Well grazed and sprightly.'

'Yes,' Hasan said. 'We have a new shepherd.'

'Where is he? I've been searching all over Tire for him.'

Hasan beckoned to me. I began to tremble. In my fear I couldn't look him in the eye.

'Come closer,' he said. 'Was it you grazing the sheep? Where are you from?'

'From Macedonia, Kosovo.'

'You seem good and capable; I'll keep you on. It's a stroke of luck you've turned up. I've been going to Tire every day to find a shepherd and returning empty-handed. What's your name?'

'Behchet,' I said.

'Good man,' he said. 'Well, you must be hungry. Come to my house.'

We set off. He on horseback, I on foot.

I thought I was being taken away to be hung.

As we passed in front of the mosque, about twenty armed *chettes* wearing bandoliers rushed out.[13] I turned pale at the sight of them.

They teased my master: 'What a shepherd you've found after seven days toing and froing in Tire!'

'Well and good,' he said to them. 'After I make my yoghurt in springtime I'll get him to wrestle you.' And he looked at my scrawny body.

'Pay no heed to what they say,' he said. And we continued on our way. When we got to his house he said to me, 'Take off your shoes and go on up.'

'I can't do that,' I said. 'I'm dirty.'

'Go on, man! Take them off and go on up.'

I took them off and placed them by the door, ready to grab them and flee.

The master had an uncle, his father's brother, whom he called to come and help him work out my payment. He then told the women to prepare food and they set the *sofra*.[14] The master washed himself, prayed and sat at the table without eating.

'Eat up, my boy,' he said. 'Don't mind me, I'm fasting. I made a vow that if the *giaours* left I would fast for three years, and the Almighty heard me.'

---

[13] (Turkish *çete*). Rebel Turkish bands who during the period from 1919 to 1922 fought as irregulars attacking the Greek army and local Greek population.

[14] (Greek σοφράς from Turkish *sofra*). A low, round table at which people, sitting on the floor or on pillows, take their meals.

'Yes,' I said. 'It was He and not our might that drove them out.'

And I lost my appetite. I ate a mouthful and sat back from the table. The others followed. They gave me some tobacco to roll a cigarette and began to ask me once more where I'd come from.

'From Aydin,' I told them. 'Looking for work.'

'You needn't worry now you're here,' they said to me. 'You'll be treated well. The Greeks have gone. We run things now.'

'Yes,' I said. 'They've gone. Let's not talk about them.'

'*Ismi rahmani rahim*.[15] In the name of God, the Merciful, the Compassionate.' And the conversation began again at the beginning.

'Are you a shepherd?' the master asked me. 'Do you know the trade well?'

'Yes,' I said. 'Try me out, master. If you find me capable, keep me on.'

'If you're what I'm looking for, you'll want for nothing. What agreement do you wish to make?'

'Let's say two months, so we get to know each other,' I said. 'Then we'll see. We can make another agreement, for a year or two years, whatever you wish.'

---

[15] The narrator is referring to words from the Muslim prayer *Bismillah irahman irahim* (In the name of God, the Merciful, the Compassionate), which begins almost every chapter of the Koran and is often uttered as a propitious invocation.

I said that because my companion and I had agreed to meet in two months.

'All right,' he said. 'We'll do it that way. How much do you want?'

'Fifty pound notes for two months,' I said. All I really wanted was food to eat.

'That's too much,' he said. 'Two hundred and fifty milkers with three shepherds. It doesn't pay. Make it less. If you're capable and skilled I'll pay you that much after the end of our first agreement. Take thirty-five for now and stay.'

'No, forty and you won't be disappointed,' I said.

'All right,' he said. 'Five pounds won't break me. Food and clothing are paid by me and you can go to town whenever you like.'

Our agreement was done.

That night they put on a feast. I enjoyed it.

'Behchet, I've forgotten myself,' the master said. 'You're tired. You'll be wanting to sleep.'

He led me to a room. He gave me a shepherd's cape and showed me some bedclothes the women had already taken there.

'Here,' he said. 'They're yours. Undress and make your bed.'

In my fear I didn't sleep a wink. I kept thinking they'd turn me in. At first light I was still wrapped in my cape.

Around dawn I heard them talking.

'Behchet,' the master called to me after a while. 'Are you awake?'

'Yes,' I said and leapt to my feet.

I washed hurriedly. We drank coffee together and set off for the fold, I on foot and he on horseback. The other shepherds were waiting for us there. The time came for us to let the sheep out of the fold. As they went out I counted three hundred, milkers and non-milkers together.

'Master,' I said before I set out, 'I'll count them every day and if any are lost I'll pay for them, and if any should die I'll bring you their hides.'

The master patted me on the back.

'Just as you said, Behchet, you're true to your word. Good for you.'

That night I milked two hundred and fifty sheep, forty-five *okas* of milk. With the morning's milk that made eighty-six. When the master came he couldn't believe it. He worked out that it was about thirty-two extra *okas* of milk.

'My!' he said. 'That's a lot of milk. You're up there with the Greeks we used to have here. You're in a class with them.'

'I'm from Kosovo,' I said. 'And in our part of the world all we have is sheep.'

'Well done!' he congratulated himself. 'I've got myself a good shepherd. I'm glad indeed.'

And he gave me some halva to eat.

Hasan complained to him that he'd been working for him for three years and had never eaten halva.

'Whoever is capable and hard-working is rewarded,' the master replied.

The Arvanites had their sheepfolds close by.

One day as I was grazing the sheep, their master lay in wait for me on the path.

'What a shame,' he said. 'You're wasting your skill. If you came and worked for me I'd have you milking only.'

'No,' I said. 'I've made an agreement. I don't break my word.' And I went on my way.

That night when he met my master he said to him, 'Where did you find such a shepherd? We'll take him off you.'

'You can have my sheep but not my shepherd,' my master replied and they fell to jesting.

Time passed. One night after the master had returned from Thira he said to me, 'Come, I have good news to tell you.'

'May it bring prosperity,' I said.

'They caught a *giaour* in Aydin. He was working for a Turk and pretending to be a Muslim.'

'Tell me about it,' I said. 'How did they catch the dog?' And my tongue caught in my throat.

'He went to the mosque to pray and didn't know how to wash himself. From this and other things the *hodja* caught on. They took him away and hung him on the spot from the big plane tree in the square.'

From the features the master described I realized it was my companion. So even before March, we came to a new agreement for fifty pound notes with the expenses his, as before.

The days went by quickly, one after the other, and I was filled with fear as the fast approached.

The first day I noticed that each shaved the hair on his chest. I did the same—I shaved my chest.

'Lord, forgive me,' I said and tears came to my eyes. That year everyone was going to fast, because the *giaour*, the enemy, had gone.

'I must observe the fast, too,' I said to the master.

'I'll fast for you,' he said to me. 'You bear no sins, you are a stranger in these parts and Allah will forgive you if you don't fast.'

'No, master, I haven't fasted in years and now that we've rid ourselves of the enemy we must all fast.'

'If you so want to, keep the fast,' he said. 'But if it gets too hard, let it go.'

At midnight when the gypsy began to beat on his drum the whole household got up. The *sofra* was prepared and we sat cross-legged around it and began slowly to eat.

At first light I left for the fold. The older shepherd and the younger apprentice had taken the sheep out and left them to graze at a distance from the hut. The two of them were praying behind a rock. I joined them, knelt and did as they did.

And so this day passed and another, and many more, until I learnt their ways and breathed more easily.

Bayram[16] was almost upon us. The master said to me one day, 'Go and get dressed up. We're going to town to shop for you. It's about time you enjoyed life like everyone else.'

'Don't trouble yourself over me, master,' I said, fearing someone might recognize me in Thira.

'No,' he said. 'Let's go and we'll buy whatever you like.'

Reluctantly I set off with him for Thira.

When we got to the bazaar, he bought me a set of clothes: breeches and jacket, a pair of leather leggings, a sash, a fez and a thick woollen turban. When I had gathered them all in my arms, he asked me, 'What else can I get you, Behchet?'

'Nothing. These are enough, master.'

'I'll buy you some Zeybek breeches.'

'No,' I said. 'We don't have time to have them sewn.'

'There are ready-made ones,' he said and strode off through the crowds.

---

[16] One of the two most important Muslim festivals. It is the breaking of the fast at the end of Ramadan.

We searched all over but couldn't find my size.

'It doesn't matter, master. Don't trouble yourself,' I said to him. 'What you've bought me is enough.'

'No, we'll buy the material,' he said. 'The women will sew them.'

Bayram came and I was terrified because I didn't know how to enter the mosque. I'd learnt everything that went on outside the mosque, but not inside.

The night before, the master said to me, 'Do the milking early so you'll be in time for the mosque.'

'Yes,' I said eagerly.

When he had gone I let the young apprentice take off to his village. Then Hasan, the shepherd, left and I remained alone.

In the morning, up rode the master on his horse.

'Where are the others?' he asked.

I told him, pretending I was worried.

'What a shame that I won't be able to worship. After all that fasting.'

'It doesn't matter,' he said. 'It can't be helped.' And he embraced me, and I hugged him tight.

'*Bayram mubarek ola!* May your Bayram be joyful!'

'*Allah erez ola*. May Allah bless it,' we wished each other.

After we pulled away he said to me, 'This has saddened me—you should have come.'

'It doesn't matter, master,' I replied. 'They're young. Let them have their fun.'

'No,' he said. 'Age comes first. Never mind, you'll have your chance when the Kurban Bayram comes.'

We said our farewells and he left.

Just before midday the young apprentice came. His name was Riza. An hour later, Hasan turned up.

After we'd chatted a while, we left Riza with the flock and went down to Thira for a stroll.

Everything was prettily decorated. In front of the garrison headquarters the flags flapped in the wind. Lots of reed pipes and drums were playing in the coffee houses. Their sound made me shiver. I remembered our own feast days and tears came to my eyes. The joy around me mingled with my own sorrow. I lost my nerve.

'Let's leave,' I said to Hasan.

He dragged me into the coffee house to buy a *lokum*.[17] Inside and outside, armed *chettes* were dancing. Their guns and knives seemed to fly through the air.

'Come on,' Hasan said to me. 'Keep moving so we can have a go.'

The coffee house keeper sat astride a chair calling out to people in turn.

'You,' he asked me. 'Are you going to dance? Go on.'

---

[17] (Greek λουκούμι from Turkish *lokum*). Turkish delight.

'No, I don't know how,' I said. 'I'm a Macedonian.'

'If you don't know how, don't come in. Now you're here, you'll dance.' And he pulled me along.

Hasan followed me and we began to dance.

'Look at the *muhajir* dancing!' they were saying around us. As I danced I noticed the gendarme patrol looking at us. I panicked.

'Let's go,' I said to Hasan. 'The boy is alone up there with a mountain of sheep.'

'No,' he said. 'We'll stay till morning.'

I left him and headed back to the fold. The master was there. He was surprised to see me.

'Why have you returned?' he asked.

And he insisted I go back.

'I'm tired, master,' I said. 'I'll go again tomorrow.'

The next day I milked the sheep early as I always did and, after putting them in the hollow with the apprentice, I returned to the fold to change. I washed, spruced myself up and headed for town.

As I passed the inn, I saw Sali Efendi, the tax collector, in front of me. He knew my family from the village because we had sheep and he had often stayed at our house.

'The dog!' I said to myself and quickly changed direction.

All that day I roamed the streets. Wherever I went I felt uneasy. I kept thinking Sali Efendi was coming up behind me.

The sun had set and I didn't have the courage to

return. Finally I dusted down my new clothes, rearranged my fez and headed back to the fold.

The sheep were grazing close by. Hasan came over to me. I didn't speak to him. I changed into my old clothes and felt calmer.

The days went by and the master was more and more kind to me.

One night as we were counting the milk he said to me, 'You know, Behchet, now that summer is coming I'm thinking of dividing the fields. On the three acres with the water pump I'll put in a melon patch. What's your opinion?'

'Whatever you decide, master. We'll need hands to help.'

'Yes,' he said. 'I know that. We'll all set to work, the women as well.'

After some days we put up the *chardak*, the makeshift hut, in the middle of the field. There were fig trees all around us. Everything was fine. The women worked hard and served us with cooked food.

During the days we worked there, the master got it into his head to marry me to one of his nieces, the daughter of his brother who had been killed in the Dardanelles.[18]

---

[18] Referring to the nine-month Gallipoli campaign during World War I, in which Turkish forces defended the Gallipoli peninsula against British, Australian and New Zealand troops.

'It's not right, master,' I said to him. 'I'm poor and a stranger. I'm not worthy to enter your house.'

'Yes,' he said. 'You are worthy. I want you to be family, to take the place of my brother Suleyman, to marry his daughter Zubeyde.'

'Master,' I said to him. 'Forgive me, but I won't remarry. I was unlucky the first time. I'm not entering society again. There's my sister, too. I've left her on her own in Bursa.'

When the women heard about our conversation from the master they fell upon me.

'We'll marry you off, Behchet. Bring your sister, too. We'll be sisters.'

'First I must go and fetch her, then one day I'll marry.'

'We'll do it that way, then,' the master said. 'But for my part I want your word.'

'All right,' I said to him. 'But first I must bring my sister, then we'll see.'

August was nearing, the end of our agreement, and I was thinking about how I would leave. For where, I didn't know. When the time came I spoke to the master.

'The government is rounding up draft dodgers and I don't have papers. I lost them in the time of the Greeks.'

'Is that what you're worrying about?' he said. 'We'll give Mustafa Efendi a lamb and you'll have them by tomorrow. Give me the names of your parents and your birthplace.'

I wrote them down on a piece of paper for him and the next morning he went down to Thira. That night when he returned he gave me my identity papers.

'Here, Behchet, take them,' he said. 'Before the end of the month we'll make an agreement for a year.'

'I'm thinking of leaving for a little while,' I said to him.

'Where are you going?' he asked, taken aback.

'I have to go to Bursa, to see my sister, as I was telling you. I've been away from home for two years and I've heard no news of her.'

'We'll send a telegram, this very night, and tomorrow you'll have an answer. I have an acquaintance in Bursa.'

'No,' I said. 'I have to go myself.'

'All right, go,' he replied, troubled. 'I'll pay all your expenses. Stay till September. If you want to come back earlier, the door of my house is always open for you.'

'If I don't die, master,' I said to him. 'I am yours.'

'Thank you,' he said to me and left.

The very next morning he went to Thira to find a shepherd.

This time he found one straight away. He brought him home. Kadir was his name. He'd been a prisoner of the Greeks and had just been released. From him I heard about the calamity that had taken place.

When the master saw I was getting ready, he gave me my money, one hundred and fifty-five pound notes. The women washed and darned my clothes. They told me to go and pick figs from the orchard and gave me some baskets to carry them with. When I returned to the house they folded my clothes, put them in a deeper basket and sewed some cloth over the top.

'Take this basket of figs as a gift to your sister,' they said. 'And tell her we're waiting for her.'

I said nothing. I couldn't find the words.

On that last night, we ate together as we had the first time and stayed up late.

I stayed awake all night, my eyes wide open. It seemed the longest night of all.

At daybreak we all got up. The sound of our footsteps was louder than our talk. The women fried pancakes with grape syrup to have with our coffee. We ate and prayed that we would soon meet again. When the moment came for me to leave I took them by the hand.

'Thank you very much,' I said. 'You've been very kind to me.'

'*Helal olsun, unutma,*' the master said. 'You deserved it. Don't forget us.'

'*Unutma*. Don't forget us,' the women said.

We said our farewells.

The master mounted his horse and I the donkey. Then we set off.

When we got to Thira we went to the inn. The innkeeper was a Macedonian, my master knew him, and he asked him to talk me into staying, seeing we were from the same parts.

'Out of the question,' I said to him. 'Once a man has chosen his path, don't turn him back.'

And I said to my master, 'Don't worry. I told you, I'll be back, if He is willing.' And I pointed up to God.

'Yes,' he said. 'You've given me your word.' And he gave me money to buy him a turban from Bursa.

The innkeeper also gave me twenty-five pound notes to buy him a crimson sash.

I took the money and put it into my purse.

Then I asked my master, 'Are my papers all right or do I have to go to the garrison headquarters to have them inspected?'

'The clerk comes by here,' he said. 'He's a young fellow, a gendarme. He's a friend.'

We waited and in a little while he came. I gave him my papers and he wrote 'Destination Bursa' on them. I didn't know if the steamships were operating.

'Here you are,' he said.

'Are they all right?' I asked him. 'Or do they still need something?'

'You can go to Baghdad on those,' he said to me. But I was still uneasy.

'Don't you trust me?' my master said to me, hurt. 'I'm an honourable man. Everyone knows me in Tire. But you, you're leaving and never coming back.'

'Only if I die, master. If I don't, you can expect me.'

The moment came for the train to depart. Its whistle blew. We clasped hands.

'Godspeed,' he said. 'You've been a good man.'

'You too, master. May God give you health.' And I left hurriedly without looking back.

I boarded the train and shrank into a corner. Opposite me two Jews and a Cretan Turk were talking about the Greeks during the occupation and about a certain Panayiotis and what he'd done.

'And now we hear that the dog is in Bandirma,' the Jews were saying, and they spoke ill of the Greeks.

I sat in a corner listening to them talk about the prisoner Panayiotis.

'We Jews have made countless petitions to see him hanged, but in Tire they don't agree.'

While they were talking the Turk saw that one of the Jews carried a pistol in his pocket.

'Hey, you miserly Jew!' he said to him, rising from his seat. 'Who are you to talk? What were you doing when we were fighting the Greeks? And now here you are carrying a pistol when we don't even have one.' And he lunged forward to take it from him.

'Take me for one of those Jews, do you?' the other one said to him and they set to.

'Watch it!' the Jew said to him. 'I'm a man of property and you'll be in trouble.'

I was having fun listening to them. By and by they set to jesting and things calmed down.

After a spell, the Cretan Turk said to him again, 'You know, you're a Jew. You shouldn't have a pistol.'

We were passing through Durali. It bordered on my village. I lay low in case a Turk from there saw me.

We finally reached Smyrna. We got off at the custom house. We all got into a line. An officer stood and inspected our papers.

'Your documents,' he said to us.

I was in a state. I still didn't believe my papers were in order. I cast my eyes about, ready to bolt. Iron bars everywhere. I stood in line and hurriedly stretched out my hand with my papers over the shoulders of two other people.

'*Buyurun*. Here, Captain,' I said.

'Wait your turn,' the people in front said and gave me dirty looks.

'Your call-up year?' the officer asked me when I reached him.

'1908,' I said.

And I was allowed through.

Outside the place swarmed with fezzes. There were handcarts lined up. The cab drivers were cracking their whips in the air. I went up to one of them.

'Are you free?'

'Yes,' he said. 'Jump in. Where to?'

'The quay,' I said. 'How much do you want?'

'Four *mejidiyes*.'[19]

'Here. Let's go.'

As we drove along, fear and joy wrestled inside me. Before I knew it we were there.

'Down you get,' the cab driver said to me. 'We're here.'

I took down my two baskets and the woollen cape, a gift from my master.

---

[19] (Turkish *mecidiye*). A Turkish silver coin first minted by Sultan Abdul-Medjid in 1844.

'Are there any hotels here?' I asked him.

'Over there.' And he pointed to one.

I thanked him and left with my belongings. I found a room easily. I left my things there and went out again for a stroll.

Along the quay, from the Turkish military headquarters on, everything was in ruins. Only around the old Hermes café had a couple of other coffee houses been repaired. I sat down in one and ordered some tea. Behind me sat two men with hats.

'Two teas!' they called out in Greek.

I couldn't believe my ears.

I listened eagerly to their conversation. They were saying, 'Some fellows at the ministry have got letters from Piraeus.'

I was about to go up to them and declare myself. I held back. In a little while they got up and left. I quickly paid and followed on their heels. Each time I was about to go up to them and speak I'd pull back.

'I won't be the one to betray myself,' I thought. 'It's better that only God and myself know my secret. Let Him bring it to an end.'

I headed for the wharf to find a boatman, to ask about a steamship for Constantinople.

A boatman noticed me and said, 'What are you looking for, lad?'

'Nothing,' I replied.

'Not wanting to sail, are you?'

'Yes,' I said.

'Where to?'

'Istanbul.'

'I'll get you on a steamship,' he said.

'You're having a poor fellow on, aren't you?' I said to him.

'No, I'm serious,' he said. 'It leaves tomorrow. An Arab steamer.'

'If you believe in God, tell me the truth: I'm a poor man. If I spend my money I'll be penniless.'

'Don't worry,' he said. 'Just look out for my number and I'll take you out for free. Which hotel are you staying at?'

'I can't remember what it's called,' I said.

I kept it from him in case I gave myself away.

'Tomorrow,' he said. 'At midday, *appunto*, on the dot. I'll take you to have your papers stamped.'

I didn't believe him and asked him again about the boat leaving for Constantinople.

'You idiot, there's a ship leaving for Istanbul every day,' he said to me.

'All right, I believe you,' I said and I went off to an eating house. I was so happy I lost my appetite. I paid the bill and went to the hotel to get some sleep. The night was endless. I tossed and turned.

At the first light of day, I got up and went down to the wharf. I found the boatman and asked him again about the ship leaving for Constantinople.

'The steamship's right under your nose and you still won't believe it?' he said. 'Get a move on.'

In my joy I started running towards the harbour-master's office.

'Wait, we'll go together,' he called out to me.

'No, don't bother,' I said. 'I'll go on my own.'

When I got there, there was a crowd lined up. I let the people pass me by and watched the clerks writing hurriedly on the papers as they handed them from one to another. I had to take my place. I shut my eyes and joined the queue.

I'd come this far. I was in God's hands now.

'Your travel warrant,' the clerk standing at the door asked me.

I gave it to him. He looked at it closely. I began to tremble.

'Your father's name?' he said.

'Suleyman,' I said.

'Your mother's name?'

'Zahire.'

'Call-up year?'

'1908.'

'Where do you live?'

'Tire.'

'It says here Kosovo.'

'That's where I'm from.'

'Where are you going now?'

'Istanbul. My family have arrived. They wrote to me to go and meet them.'

'Where have they come from?'

'Serbia.'

'There are troubles in Istanbul. Why don't you wait until they're over?'

'I can't,' I said. 'I'm a poor man. If I wait two days, I'll have spent all my money.'

'All right,' he said. 'When you get to Istanbul, go to Birlar Street. There's a fellow there. I've ordered some boots from him. It's been two months and he still hasn't sent them. Give him this card and tell him to hurry up and send them.'

'Of course,' I said. 'Rest assured.'

And I went to the major to have my travel warrant stamped.

I left the place running. I took my things from the hotel and headed straight for the boatman.

There, someone checked my papers again.

'Okay,' he said. 'You're free to go.'

Then the boatman took me. At the ship someone else looked at my papers again.

'You're free to go,' he said, too.

I climbed up onto the steamship, turning my back so I wouldn't see behind me. I asked a young man when we were leaving.

'In five minutes,' he said.

And we were soon underway.

On the ship were Turkish civilians bound for Constantinople. Next to me a group of them were eating and singing in high spirits. It was getting dark. In the far distance the lights of Mytilini were visible like tiny candles. The Turks, men, women and children, were saying spitefully, 'We'll see that *esek Midili* again, that big ass Mytilini!'

They were hoping that the ship wouldn't call in to the port so they wouldn't have to see the *giaours* again.[20]

An old man was standing a little apart from them, listening to them gloomily. He had sailed from Alexandria. I approached him to start a conversation. He didn't look like a Turk.

He scowled at me. I drew back.

After a while I approached him again.

'Why won't you talk to me?' I asked in Turkish.

'What do you want with me?' he said.

'I wanted to ask you something. Will the ship be berthing at Mytilini?'

'How would I know?' he answered.

'Where are you going anyway?'

'Why do you ask?' he said.

'You look Greek to me. I'm Greek too. I've been inside Turkey for a year now. I made out I was a Turk to save myself.'

'You don't say!' he said to me in Greek.

---

[20] Greece and Turkey were no longer at war. The peace Treaty of Lausanne had been signed and a compulsory population exchange had been agreed by the Greek and Turkish governments. At the time, the process of moving refugees and prisoners of war was ongoing.

'I swear on the cross,' I said and made the sign of the cross secretly so no one else would see.

'Forgive me,' he said. 'When you spoke to me I was saying to myself, "What does this dirty dog want." Stay here. I'll go and see the steward. He's Greek, too. We'll see what can be done.'

He went and spoke to him.

'There's a Christian on board dressed as a Turk. He's come from Smyrna. We must save him.'

'Who is he?'

The old man brought him over and pointed to me. 'That's him.'

The steward said to me in a low voice, 'Follow me.' And he took me to his cabin.

'I'm an Anatolian, too,' he said.[21]

'If you're an Anatolian, save me.'

'So you're a Christian? How did you manage to escape?'

I told him my story quickly, trembling as I did so.

'You needn't be afraid any more,' he said.

He went to the English captain and told him.

The captain also came and he spoke to me in broken Greek.

'Greek?'

---

[21] Anatolian Greeks, also known as Asia Minor Greeks, were a significant minority in Turkey and had a different cultural identity to the Greeks who lived within Greece's national borders before 1922.

'Yes, Greek.'

'How was it the Turks didn't cut off your head?'

'It was God's will,' I answered him.

'*Bono, bono*,' he said and gave me a cigarette.

'I'm in your hands now,' I said. 'God has handed me over to you. I've been through a lot. Don't take me to Constantinople. I'd rather die here.'

The ship began sounding its siren as it slowly dropped anchor in Mytilini harbour. The harbourmaster came aboard. The steward whispered the news in his ear.

'Which one?' he asked with a gesture.

'That one over there,' and the steward pointed to me.

'You don't say! That Mehmet?'

I was keeping an eye on the ship in case it got underway again.

'Come over here,' the steward said to me. 'Show us your papers.'

I handed them over.

'What? Turkish? Don't you have European papers?' the harbourmaster said. 'I don't know who you are. I can't take you off.'

'I'm Greek and if you don't take me I'll drown myself right here in front of you.'

He wouldn't budge.

'Why won't you believe me?' I said.

'If I believed everyone so easily the law would hang me.'

'Take me and put me in jail,' I said. 'Interrogate me.'

'I can't do that. It's not my job.'

The ship was weighing anchor, ready to leave. The harbourmaster was climbing down the ladder.

The steward said to him, 'Why don't you send a sailor to the garrison to ask the commander?'

'Well, that would change things. Someone else would be responsible.' And he sent someone to ask.

The order came for me to be taken under escort.

'Go on, off you go,' the harbourmaster said. 'You're out of my hands.'

I took off my fez and hid it. The Turks stared at us as we climbed down to the boat.

We landed at the harbourmaster's office. As we walked along the waterfront there were refugees at the municipal garden waiting to leave for Macedonia.[22] When they heard my story there was a commotion, as everyone, men and women, crowded around me. We went inside a coffee house and it filled with people. Everyone was trying to catch my eye, asking me if I had news of their families.

'I can't tell you anything,' I said. 'I was in the mountains for a year, hiding in caves.'

---

[22] Macedonia refers to the large region of the same name in northern Greece where many Greek refugees from Turkey settled after 1922.

After I drank my tea, which was paid for by my guard, I was taken to the garrison.

As soon as the garrison commander saw me he said, 'Welcome. Sit down.' He asked me where I was from, where I was going, where I did my military service and who my commander was.[23]

I told him everything.

'Is there anyone from Sokia[24] here that you know?'

'How would I know?' I said. 'I've just arrived.'

'Don't you know anyone?' he asked the gendarmes.

'There's a hotelkeeper, sir,' one of them said. 'I think he's from Sokia.'

'Take him over there. If they know each other, he can stay at the hotel. If no one knows him, bring him back.'

I looked at him.

'I'm sorry, my boy,' he said. 'I have no choice.'

'You're right,' I said. 'I was a soldier, too. I know about duty.'

'You can go,' he said to us.

When we got to the hotel the gendarme called out to the keeper.

---

[23] The narrator, as well as serving in the Ottoman Army in World War I, must have also enlisted in the Greek army between 1919 and 1922.

[24] (Turkish Sökia). Town about 80 kilometres south of Smyrna and not far from the narrator's village of Kirkidze. In 1922, Sokia had about 7,000 Greek and 9,000 Turkish inhabitants.

'Aleko! Aleko! Come here. I've brought you a fellow countryman.'

The hotelkeeper came.

'What do you mean, a fellow countryman?' he said. 'This man's a bloody Turk!'

And he looked me up and down.

'Come on, we're from the same parts,' I said to him. 'Come closer. You won't catch anything. I'm not a Turk.'

'He's from around Aydin,' the gendarme said. 'From Kirkidze.'

'Name me one man from Kirkidze,' the hotelkeeper said to me.

'Liberis, the richest man in our village.'

'Put it there,' he said and we slapped our palms together in a friendly shake.

'May I go?' the gendarme asked him.

'Yes, he'll stay with me tonight. I'll take responsibility. Come and fetch him in the morning.'

We talked about our troubles till midnight. Sleep overcame us as we talked.

I awoke in the morning feeling calmer. I dressed and went to the church. I lit a candle, knelt and prayed. When I got back to the hotel the gendarme was there.

'Let's go,' he said.

And off we went to the garrison and from there to the prefecture. They issued me with documents and sent me with an escort to Piraeus.

When we sailed into Chios, on the quay I saw some fellow villagers. As I looked at the crowd I saw my own family who were leaving that very day for Kozani.

When he'd finished telling his story, I said to him, 'Sign your name.'
And he wrote:

Nikolas Kozakoglou

BACKGROUND NOTE
BY THE AUTHOR

Towards the end of my first journalistic tour[25] (September to December 1928) I had visited some refugee settlements in the Katerini area. In my notes I had been writing 'It's raining, raining, raining. Soon I'll be back in the city. I must complete my mission well. It's almost at an end but an important part is yet to come. I'm about to speak to people who've suffered and are destitute. May God be with me and help me.'

I paused from my notes at this point and I went down to the coffee house in the refugee village of Stoupi (Spi) to meet with people and hear their troubles. The coffee house was packed. In the thick smoke I listened and took notes. 'Long-term loans. Land reclamation. The refugee settlement requests

---

[25] Doukas made two such tours in northern Greece in 1928 and 1929.

the winding up of accounts and the filing of annual returns. Refugee settlement orders, debtors' warrants, taxes. You weep and the officials laugh... our troubles are many.'

The latch on the door rattled and a man entered. He was of medium height, broad-chested with fair hair and blue eyes. I made a sketch of him. Everyone shouted together, 'That's the one who made out he was a Turk to save himself.' A Turk to save himself? I pricked up my ears like a cavalry horse on hearing the call of a bugle. I prepared myself to hear something incredible, but this shy Anatolian blushed and sat down in a corner without speaking. But in a while, with some ouzo and conversation, he warmed up. He began his story; he spoke Turkish like all of them, but as a storyteller was a real Anatolian. It was as if he was playing a violin solo for me. Totally absorbed, we all fell silent.

Halfway through, I could see that I had to retain this story. I began to take notes again. I soon captured his rhythm. A Turkish speaker as he was, he put his verbs at the end. 'Good, I said, he is.' This foreign and paratactic syntax with its oft-repeated conjunctive 'and' brought to mind the style of the Old Testament. In intense excitement, heightened by haste, I preserved, omitted and changed words. I also changed their somewhat corrupted rhythm, shifting it to a classical epic narrative and speech. When he had finished his narration I really did say to him, 'Sign your name.'

He signed 'Nikolas Kazakoglou' (I changed the name to 'Kozakoglou' for greater effect).[26]

The next morning I went to his house, where I met his young wife and child, and I asked him to dictate the beginning of the story which I hadn't written down. But his narrative no longer had the same warmth. This is why in the first two editions the beginning is hurried. I got him to write a letter in Turkish to Hadji Mehmet, that wonderful man who had displayed such true folk kindness. In it he explained how Behchet who had once worked for him was a Greek who was now in his new country, and he thanked him for the kindness he had shown him. He ended by saying that 'those who know the world know that all these things are the work of God'. (I kept a copy of the letter in Turkish and one in translation.)

When I left the village on my way to Katerini I felt that I was holding a piece of gold in my hand. For a fleeting moment, I felt the friendly touch of an enormous palm on my shoulder as though God himself were favouring me with a blessing and mainstay for the rest of my days.

I spent Christmas at Kitros and on New Year's Eve returned to Thessaloniki.[27] I began writing straight

---

[26] The 'greater effect' may relate to the fact that the Greek word for Cossacks, people noted for their fierce independence and military skill, is Kozaki.

[27] Kitros is a village between Katerini and Thessaloniki. In 1929,

away, dictating the story in a week.[28] Along with my 'brigand' pieces, which I was writing in instalments, I intended it for the provincial newspaper of Thessaloniki, *Makedonia*, which had commissioned my travels.[29] However, we couldn't agree on the payment and I came to Athens and gave my brigand pieces to the newspaper *Proia* and my *Prisoner of War's Story* to the publisher H. Ganiaris.

The next year (1929), when I set out on my second tour—this time to paint, not to write—I called by the village of Spi and took Nikolas and his companion a copy of their published story. As Nikolas read it he laughed contentedly and marvelled that it was exactly how he had said it. His companion who was tall and dark (like a Cretan Turk), a stutterer and a timid man (which was why he was caught and imprisoned in Smyrna from where he was freed) was troubled by the fact that I'd had him hung in my story. 'B...b...but

---

Doukas, himself a refugee, was living temporarily in Thessaloniki with his mother and sister.

[28] Doukas didn't physically write the narrative himself but, using his notes as his source, dictated it to his cousin Andreas Hatzidimitriou in Thessaloniki in January 1929.

[29] The brigand pieces were a series of journalistic articles on the harsh conditions of communities in the mountain areas in the western Macedonian region. They were published in the newspaper *Proia* from 3 to 11 March 1929 under the title 'The Brigand Society' ('Η ληστρική κοινωνία'), which was the editor's title. Doukas's original title was 'Life in the Greek Mountains' ('Η ορεινή Ελλάδα').

w...w...why d...d...did y...y...you have me killed?' he said to me. How could I answer? That the story demanded it? He wouldn't have understood.

Before departing I left Nikolas enough paper to write down his story himself; he did sit down and write it and, years later, brought it to me in Athens. It would have been around 1933–34 (because in the meantime I had published the second edition in 1932). But his writing wasn't as good as his oral account; the best passages were those he copied word for word from the book. But he did add some episodes which I used in the third edition. I deposited Nikolas's manuscript of his story in the Corfu library. I trust it's still there.

In the third edition I changed the basic shape of the book. While retaining and emphasizing the vernacular, I rid it of its primitivistic elements, its exaggerations and repetitions, even slowing its rhythm, so that the narrative voice would have greater ease and breathing space. And so, though the text did lose some of its expressive charm, it became more solid and durable. In the same way, I consolidated the structure with a classical division of the story into four parts, each self-sufficient but also a part of a unity (the first, from capture to escape with his companion; the second, reaching their village where they live as outcasts and cave dwellers; the third, the height of their desperation, decision to separate and go out and work as Turks; and the fourth, the hero's escape and redemption). Consequently the text gained in variety and unity and the story became more enduring.

Variety and unity were also achieved through the strict application of another classical principle, that of oppositions and dramatic climax, which operate from the very beginning with the capture and confinement of Nikolas and his companion in the garrison, through the presence of the clerk who observes everything and the cavalry captain who forces them to kneel as he counts them, through their public pillorying in the marketplace and the presence of the *hafiz* and, finally, the *efe* from their village in whose presence they 'fell to the ground so he wouldn't recognize [them]'. The material was structured in this oppositional way from beginning to end. In addition, the story contains a further classical principle, that of 'the beginning, middle and end'. This classical casting of the folk material gives it a peculiarity that has given rise to a comparison, not entirely inapt, with the poet Kalvos.[30]

I will not attempt any further analysis of the intentions and achievements of my *Prisoner of War's Story*. I, like its friends, hope that it will live on.[31]

---

[30] Andreas Kalvos (1792–1869). A major modern Greek poet whose small body of poetry (twenty highly formal poems, *Odes*) deals mostly with the Greek War of Independence.

[31] This text was included as an epilogue from the 1980 Greek edition onwards.

AFTERWORD

The Asia Minor Disaster of 1922[*] and the subsequent compulsory exchange of populations between Greece and Turkey has produced a number of narratives by Anatolian Greeks. The area around Ayvali (in Turkish, Ayvalik) on the Asia Minor coast is the hub of the so-called 'Aeolian School' of the Greek prose writers. *A Prisoner of War's Story* is the inaugurating text together with *Life in the Tomb* (1930, serialized earlier in Mytilini 1923–4) by Stratis Myrivilis and Elias Venezis's *Number 31328* (1931). The refugee experience became central to the early work of these writers, who introduced the narrative of testimony into Greek

---

[*] This refers to the Asia Minor Campaign (the Greek–Turkish War of 1919–22) in which Greece tried to extend its then borders to include sizable Greek populations in the defeated Ottoman Empire. The Campaign ended in a crushing defeat for the Greek army and was followed by an influx of a million and a half Greek refugees into Greece. This traumatic and dislocating event is a watershed in twentieth-century Greek consciousness.

literature and sought to convey through it the horrors of war and captivity. Loss, pain, and lyricism permeate the narratives of these three writers whose lives were marked by war and uprootedness.

Doukas's story is one of the shortest and most powerful accounts of the ordeal of those who were unable to escape in time across the Aegean to mainland Greece. It remains one of the most widely-read stories in Greece. Acclaimed for its oral simplicity and captivating narrative qualities, it is the story of Nikolas Kozakoglou, a refugee from the Smyrna area, recorded by the author himself in the village of Stoupi (now known as New Ephesus) near Katerini. Kozakoglou escaped death by pretending to be a Muslim. His story is one of survival, not heroism, hatred or revenge. No blame is apportioned for the disaster. It is a testimony to sheer human versatility and resilience and indirectly reveals how, although Greeks and Turks lived together on the whole peacefully in earlier times, they also remained deeply ignorant and suspicious of each other's religious practices.

A Prisoner of War's Story can be seen as an episode of a larger epic, blurring the distinction between fact and fiction, legend and history. The story focuses almost exclusively on the protagonist's ordeal with little reference to the wider context, as if the narrative is divested of its historicity. It starts rather abruptly with his capture and ends similarly with his successful escape, creating the sense that the narrative is just an incident, a detail of a wider picture which is missing. In the beginning Kozakoglou belongs to a group of war prisoners, but later, his story, a personal struggle for survival and freedom, becomes predominant. This emphasis on the individuality of the main character brings out the distinctiveness of narrative voice and the singularity of style.

Doukas's narrative highlights the contrast between primitive innocence and cultural intervention, human solidarity and national identity. He maps out the transition from ethnicity to nationalism and from oral storytelling to authorial literacy. His story has been hailed by critics as a monument of orality, bearing the vestiges of a tradition going back to Xenophon's *Anabasis of Cyrus*, ancient tragedy, folktales and the *martyrologia* (lives of martyrs). By presenting momentous events in deceptively simple words, and avoiding descriptions, epithets or other embellishments, the story relies on its overwhelming directness. Almost devoid of emotions or judgements, Doukas's story consists of bare events related dispassionately by the protagonist Nikolas Kozakoglou.

The writer assumes the role of a mere recorder, but one can sense a conscious effort to turn the account into fiction. Doukas acts as a phonographer in a way similar to that in which his hero acts as a Muslim in order to escape death. He Hellenizes and purifies the oral account of Kozakoglou, who being a native Turkish speaker, is heavily influenced by Turkish syntax and vocabulary. Hence, the story is not a transcript of Kozakoglou's account, but a reworking by the writer himself. Wearing masks and switching identities, it blends the horrors of captivity subtly with the illusion of story-telling. The story works as a mask within a mask in an almost narcissistic manner. The narrator wore a mask to pass himself off as a Muslim while the writer Doukas wears a mask to create the fictional narration. Story and discourse, author and protagonist are linked inextricably as the former follows the survival tactics of the latter. The story is as much about shedding artistic devices and enabling the faces to 'speak' for themselves as it is about hiding behind thinly disguised identities and masks. It thrives on its duplicity and pretence by stressing its status as a truthful account and at the same time flaunting its construction. The narrator's friend, for example, survived in reality whereas in the story he is caught and hung.

A number of textual changes of ideological significance occur in the 1958 third edition of the novel in which the patriotism of the captives is enhanced while the references to their selfishness or cowardice, indicated by their cheers for Kemal Ataturk, are omitted. Significantly, the dedication of the first and second editions (dedicated to the common ordeals of the Greek and Turkish people) was changed in the third to: 'dedicated to the common ordeals of people everywhere'. This might be due to the subsequent experience of the Second World War or could be accounted for by the writer's socialist beliefs.

Although Doukas's story enjoyed a considerable reputation among Greek critics and readers, it is difficult to claim a direct influence on any particular writer.

It formed, however, together with General Makriyannis's *Memoirs* a formidable model of oral simplicity and stylistic economy for younger writers such as Thanassis Valtinos, Hronis Missios, Sotiris Dimitriou and others. From the 1960s onwards, they published stories which revived the narratives of testimony and the oral immediacy of Makriyannis and Doukas. These stories highlight the connection berween literature and truth. Unfolding different kinds of drama—of post-independence Greece (Makriyannis), of captivity (Doukas), of civil war and emigration (Valtinos), of political imprisonment (Missios) or of the forced separation of a family after the closure of borders (Dimitriou)—these narratives do not simply demand the emotional involvement of the reader, but through their unvarnished style make claims to truth.

Thus, they strive to establish a link berween bare words, raw experience and naked truth, opposing the notion of literature relying on imagination, fictionality and stylistic inventiveness. In short, these stories put forward a different conception of literature which negates the mediation of language in conveying experience, though it is ironic that their writers are more valued for their language and storytelling skills than for the stories themselves. Doukas himself in a note on the writing of the story highlights the medium when he describes how he took notes from Kozakoglou's oral testimony and then dictated the story orally to his cousin. Nevertheless, the text maintains the illusion of oral immediacy and conceals its artful re-creation.

Doukas treats his story both as a documentary account of captivity and as a folk treasure. During the 1920s there was a growing interest among Greek writers, painters and architects in folk art, illustrated in the work and activities of Stratis Doukas and Fotis Kontoglou (also from Ayvali). It was thought that through the exploration of folk art and culture a channel of communication with the genuine, unspoilt core of human nature could be established. The naiveness of folk art was believed to express the primordial desire of humanity for peaceful coexistence and solidarity. Within this context, we can understand the attempts by Doukas and Kontoglou to transcend the social and the national in order to discover through folk craft and storytelling the primitive innocence of humanity before it was destroyed by nationalism, industrialism and war.

In his preface to the early editions Doukas exhorts his readers to collect similar stories which he describes as 'valuable mosaics which will decorate the new Greek spiritual temple'. The story is treated as 'a beautiful folk flower of oral discourse' and not so much as a historical monument. His initial aim appears to be the initiation of a project similar to that of the folklorist N.G. Politis who in the 1880s instigated the collection of folk material and laid the foundations of folklore scholarship as a study of the national heritage. Doukas's recording of the story seems to be motivated by his interest in folk craftsmanship and the primitivist tendencies of his own period. The omission of this preface in subsequent editions (from the fifth edition of 1969 onwards) signals a change in the treatment of the story by the author and his audience. It could be argued that the story has gradually gained in national and historical importance over the years without losing its charm as a narrative.

Stratis Doukas was born on 6 May 1895 on the Moschonisia islands (the main island is called today Alibey in Turkish). He went to the secondary school at Ayvali together with the writer and painter Fotis Kontoglou. In 1912 he enrolled in the Law Faculty at Athens University, but at the outbreak of the First World War he abandoned his studies. Attracted by its monastic life, he paid his first visit to Mount Athos in 1914 where he would later spend a year (1923–4) with the painter Spyros Papaloukas as part of their aesthetic quest and artistic explorations. During the period 1916--17 he served as a volunteer in the army of National Defence* and later took part in battles on the Macedonian (1917–18) and Anatolian (1919–22) fronts, where he was wounded.

When in 1923 he returned to civilian life after seven years in the army, Doukas became the artistic director of a commercial venture to introduce traditional Anatolian crafts such as pottery and carpet weaving into Greece. After a few years he became seriously ill and

---

* An organization set up by Venizelist officers and politicians in 1916 with the ostensible aim of defending newly-won Greek Macedonia from the Bulgarians.

moved to Thessaloniki to be close to his family. Following his recovery, he travelled in the countryside of western Macedonia from September to December 1928 as a reporter for the newspaper *Makedonia* and it was during these travels that he met Kozakoglou and wrote his story.

Following his younger brother Alekos who had moved to Australia ten years earlier, his mother, sister and her husband emigrated to Australia in 1937. His mother died there two years later. The years up to 1936 were the most crucial and fruitful for him as a writer and artist. Afterwards, his involvement in social and political activities prevented him from concentrating on his creative work.

During the Second World War, Doukas settled permanently in Athens where he married Dimitra Diakaki. Encouraged by him, Dimitra turned to writing. In the 1950s he served as a secretary of the Society of Greek Authors and contributed articles and art reviews to journals and newspapers. He became a member of the Communist party and his political beliefs caused him trouble during the military dictatorship (1967–74). In 1962 he went to Moscow to have an operation which, however, was not carried out. After this time he remained confined at home. Doukas died on 26 November 1983.

Following his *Prisoner of War's Story*, Doukas wrote a number of short, mostly lyrical, literary texts (*Enotia* 1974, nine prose pieces written during the 1930s and 1940s, *Thermokipio* 1982), travel notes (*Odoiporos*, published in 1968, but written around 1929) and studies on art and artists (Yannoulis Halepas, Spyros Papaloukas). He also published a collection of drawings (1979). It should be noted that most of his texts are accompanied by drawings either by him or others, demonstrating how word and image were intertwined for Doukas. He was also involved in the publication of a number of journals, including the influential modernist journal *The Third Eye* (1935–7).

However, his reputation as a writer rests exclusively on *A Prisoner of War's Story* which, so far, has passed through almost thirty editions. It was first published in March 1929 and was reprinted in 1932, 1958, 1962 (in Bucharest), 1969 (in Thessaloniki), and 1977 (with drawings by Dimitris Mytaras). The seventh edition, with drawings by the Swedish painter Bengi Kristenson, came out in 1980, and the subsequent editions are based on this one. From 1980 up to the present time it has seen almost twenty reprints, a sign of its lasting and growing popularity.

DIMITRIS TZIOVAS

MODERN GREEK CLASSICS

The MODERN GREEK CLASSICS series highlights the most significant Greek writers, poets, and works of literature since the nineteenth century in translation—a tour of different forms, authors and periods of modern Greek literature.

aiorabooks.com

C.P. CAVAFY
Selected Poems BILINGUAL EDITION
Translated by David Connolly

Cavafy is by far the most translated and well-known Greek poet internationally. Whether his subject matter is historical, philosophical or sensual, Cavafy's unique poetic voice is always recognizable by its ironical, suave, witty and world-weary tones.

STRATIS DOUKAS
A Prisoner of War's Story
Translated by Petro Alexiou
With an Afterword by Dimitris Tziovas

A classic tale of survival in a time of nationalist conflict, *A Prisoner of War's Story* is a beautifully crafted and pithy narrative. Affirming the common humanity of peoples, it earns its place among Europe's finest anti-war literature of the post-WWI period.

ODYSSEUS ELYTIS 1979 NOBEL PRIZE FOR LITERATURE
In the Name of Luminosity and Transparency
With an Introduction by Dimitris Daskalopoulos

The poetry of Odysseus Elytis owes as much to the ancients and Byzantium as to the surrealists of the 1930s, bringing romantic modernism and structural experimentation to Greece. Collected here are the two speeches Elytis gave on his acceptance of the 1979 Nobel Prize for Literature.

NIKOS ENGONOPOULOS
**Cafés and Comets After Midnight
and Other Poems** BILINGUAL EDITION
Translated by David Connolly

Derided for his innovative and, at the time, often incomprehensible modernist experiments, Engonopoulos is today regarded as one of the most original artists of his generation. In both his painting and poetry, he created a peculiarly Greek surrealism, a blending of the Dionysian and Apollonian.

M. KARAGATSIS
Junkermann
Translated by Patricia Barbeito

A modernist, picaresque epic, set in the interwar period, *Junkermann* recounts the life and times of a hedonistic Finnish nobleman with a checkered past who serves as a Cossack guard in the Czar's army, flees the Bolshevik revolution, and seeks his fortune as he finally settles in Greece..

M. KARAGATSIS
The Great Chimera
Translated by Patricia Barbeito

A psychological portrait of a young French woman, Marina, who marries a sailor and moves to the island of Syros. Her fate grows entwined with that of the boats and when economic downturn arrives, it brings passion, life and death in its wake.

KOSTAS KARYOTAKIS
Ballad for the Unsung Poets of the Ages
BILINGUAL EDITION

Translated by Simon Darragh

Karyotakis is the poet most emblematic of the turbulent interwar period in Greece. His poetry is often pessimistic and bitingly satirical. His writing combines reverie with sarcasm, a stifling sense of everyday reality with poignant irony. This is verse that is both piercing and resonant.

ANDREAS LASKARATOS
Reflections
BILINGUAL EDITION

Translated by Simon Darragh

Andreas Laskaratos was a writer and poet, a social thinker and, in many ways, a controversialist. His *Reflections* sets out, in a series of calm, clear and pithy aphorisms, his uncompromising and finely reasoned beliefs on morality, justice, personal conduct, power, tradition, religion and government.

MARGARITA LIBERAKI
The Other Alexander
Translated by Willis Barnstone and Elli Tzalopoulou Barnstone

A tyrannical father leads a double life; he has two families and gives the same first names to both sets of children. The half-siblings meet, love, hate, and betray one another. Hailed by Albert Camus as "true poetry," Liberaki's sharp, riveting prose consolidates her place in European literature.

ALEXANDROS PAPADIAMANDIS
Fey Folk
Translated by David Connolly

Alexandros Papadiamandis holds a special place in the history of Modern Greek letters, but also in the heart of the ordinary reader. *Fey Folk* follows the humble lives of quaint, simple-hearted folk living in accordance with centuries-old traditions, described here with both reverence and humour.

ALEXANDROS RANGAVIS
The Notary
Translated by Simon Darragh

A mystery set on the island of Cephalonia, this classic work of Rangavis is an iconic tale of suspense and intrigue, love and murder. *The Notary* is Modern Greek literature's contribution to the tradition of early crime fiction, alongside E.T.A. Hoffman, Edgar Allan Poe and Wilkie Collins.

EMMANUEL ROÏDES
Pope Joan
Translated by David Connolly

This satirical novel, a masterpiece of modern Greek literature, retells the legend of a female pope as a disguised criticism of the Orthodox Church of the nineteenth century. It was a bestseller across Europe at its time and the controversy it provoked led to the swift excommunication of its author.

ANTONIS SAMARAKIS
The Flaw
Translated by Simon Darragh

A man is seized from his afternoon drink at the Cafe Sport by two agents of the Regime by car toward Special Branch Headquarters, and the interrogation that undoubtedly awaits him there. Part thriller and part political satire, *The Flaw* has been translated into more than thirty languages.

DIONYSIS SAVVOPOULOS
The Rock Song of our Tomorrow   BILINGUAL EDITION
Translated by David Connolly

Singer-songwriter Dionysis Savvopoulos enjoys an almost mythical status with the Greek public. His language is highly inventive, often zany and surrealistic, and its inherent poetical quality has not been lost on the critics, who classify him among the other leading Greek poets of his generation.

GEORGE SEFERIS   1979 NOBEL PRIZE FOR LITERATURE
Novel and Other Poems   BILINGUAL EDITION
Translated by Roderick Beaton

Often compared during his lifetime to T.S. Eliot, Seferis is noted for his spare, laconic, dense and allusive verse. Seferis better than any other writer expresses the dilemma experienced by his countrymen then and now: how to be at once Greek and modern.

ILIAS VENEZIS
Serenity
Translated by Joshua Barley

The novel follows the journey of a group of Greek refugees from Asia Minor who settle in a village near Athens. It details the hatred of war, the love of nature that surrounds them, the hostility of their new neighbours and eventually their adaptation to a new life.

GEORGIOS VIZYENOS
Thracian Tales
Translated by Peter Mackridge

These short stories bring to life Vizyenos' native Thrace. Through masterful psychological portrayals, each story keeps the reader in suspense to the very end: Where did Yorgis' grandfather travel on his only journey? What was Yorgis' mother's sin? Who was responsible for his brother's murder?

GEORGIOS VIZYENOS
Moskov Selim
Translated by Peter Mackridge

A novella by Georgios Vizyenos, one of Greece's best-loved writers, set in Thrace during the time of the Russo-Turkish War, whose outcome would decide the future of southeastern Europe. *Moskov Selim* is a moving tale of kinship, despite the gulf of nationality and religion.

NIKIFOROS VRETTAKOS
Selected Poems   BILINGUAL EDITION
Translated by David Connolly

The poems of Vrettakos are rooted in the Greek landscape and coloured by the Greek light, yet their themes and sentiment are ecumenical. His poetry offers a vision of the paradise that the world could be, but it is also imbued with an awareness of the abyss that the world threatens to become.

AN ANTHOLOGY
Greek Folk Songs   BILINGUAL EDITION
Translated by Joshua Barley

The Greek folk songs were passed down from generation to generation in a centuries-long oral tradition, lasting until the present. Written down at the start of the nineteenth century, they became the first works of modern Greek poetry, playing an important role in forming the country's modern language and literature.

AN ANTHOLOGY
Greek Folk Tales
Translated by Alexander Zaphiriou

Greek folk tales, as recounted throughout Greek-speaking regions, span the centuries from early antiquity up to our times. These are wondrous, whimsical stories about doughty youths and frightful monsters, resourceful maidens and animals gifted with human speech, and they capture the temperament and ethos of the Greek folk psyche.

AN ANTHOLOGY
Rebetika: Songs from the Old Greek Underworld
BILINGUAL EDITION

Translated by Katharine Butterworth & Sara Schneider

The songs in this book are a sampling of the urban folk songs of Greece during the first half of the twentieth century. Often compared to American blues, rebetika songs are the creative expression of people living a marginal and often underworld existence on the fringes of established society.